CW00646384

DIESELS in the

EAST MIDLANDS

Plate 1: Class 45 'Peak' No. 45017 approaches Old Leake, between Thorpe Culvert and Boston, with the 11.07 (SO) Skegness to Sheffield service, on 1st August 1981.
Paul D. Shannon

Plate 2: On 12th April 1984, Class 56 No. 56120 negotiates the new trackwork at Boughton Junction with the 7G33 merry-go-round empties from High Marnham to Bevercotes.

Paul D. Shannon

DIESELS
in the
EAST MIDLANDS

Paul Shannon

Oxford Publishing Company

Copyright © 1985 Oxford Publishing Co.

ISBN 0-86093-302-4

All rights reserved. No part of this book may be reproduced or transmitted in any form or by any means, electronic or mechanical, including photocopying, recording or any information storage and retrieval system, without permission in writing from the Publisher.

Typesetting by:
Aquarius Typesetting Services, New Milton, Hants.

Printed in Great Britain by:
Netherwood Dalton & Co. Ltd., Huddersfield, Yorks.

Published by:
Oxford Publishing Co.
Link House
West Street
POOLE, Dorset

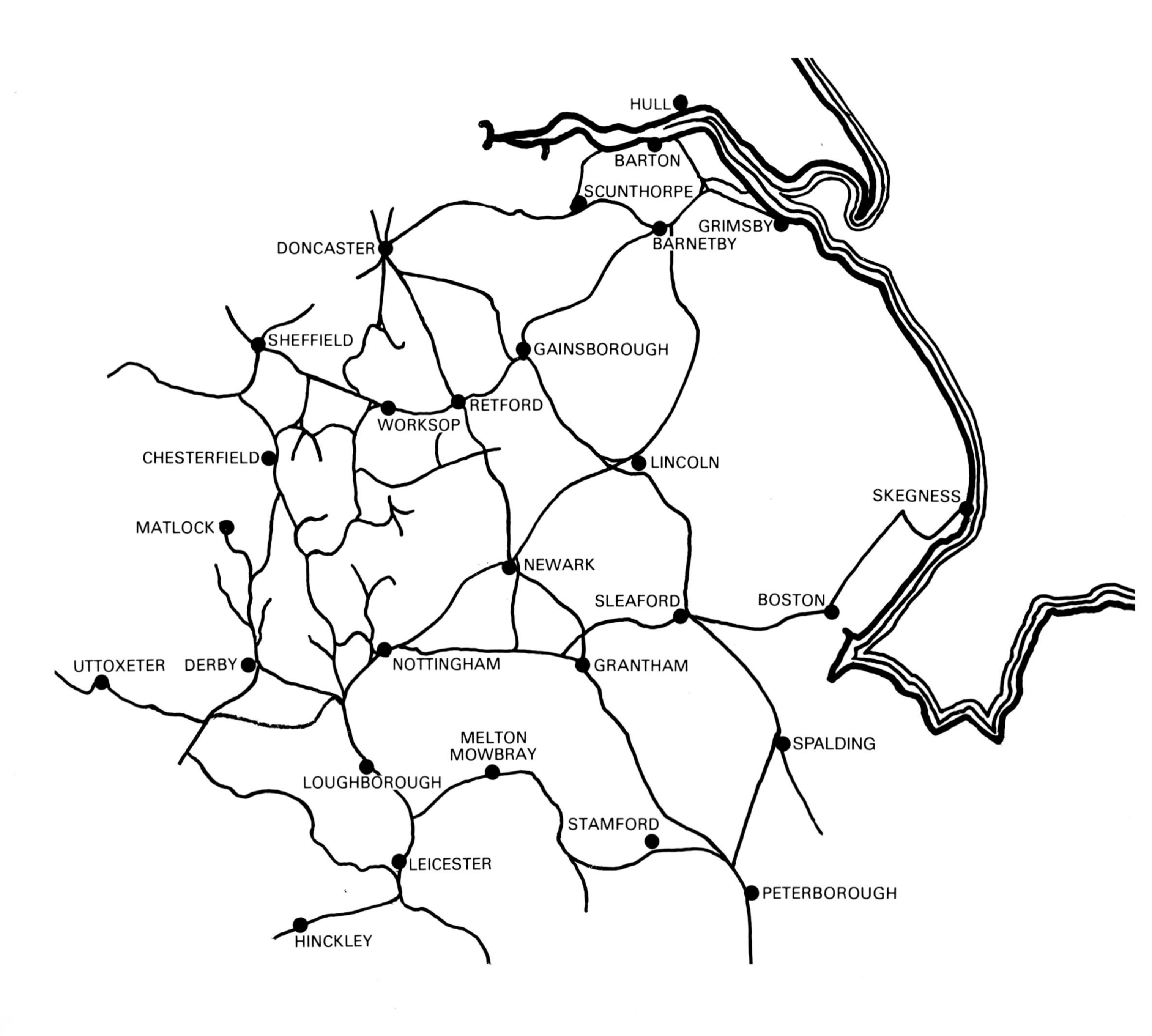

Introduction

The accompanying map shows the extent of the current railway network in the East Midlands — a network which ranges from the dense grid of lines around the Nottinghamshire/Derbyshire Coalfield, many of them freight only, to the much sparser pattern of routes across the flat and largely rural county of Lincolnshire.

Whilst the East Coast Main Line is rightly regarded as one of British Rail's key passenger routes, its importance is not greatly felt in the area covered in this volume, since relatively few trains actually serve the towns of Grantham, Newark and Retford. The Midland main line is, of course, a very different matter, since it provides the link between Leicester, Derby, Nottingham and Chesterfield, all of them important sources of traffic. Now that the High Speed Train is the principal workforce on both these main lines, the locomotive-hauled passenger train is a comparatively rare sight, apart from the three return workings on the Harwich-Nottingham-Glasgow group of services. Some compensation has been offered in recent years, however, by the introduction of Class 31-hauled formations on three of the area's more important cross-country routes — Norwich to Birmingham, Cleethorpes to Newark and, most recently, Cleethorpes to Manchester. Elsewhere, services are still mainly diesel multiple unit-operated, with the Swindon Class 120 units featuring prominently on the London Midland Region and Derby Class 114 units on the Eastern Region.

Coal provides the major source of freight traffic in the area, most of it travelling direct from colliery to power-station in merry-go-round trains. Virtually all the power-stations lie along the course of the River Trent, at West Burton, Cottam, High Marnham, Staythorpe, Ratcliffe, Castle Donington and Willington. Another important destination for coal is Immingham Docks, where there is a scheduled total of 24 arrivals and departures each day from the Yorkshire and Nottinghamshire coalfields. Very little wagonload coal traffic survives today, and the once busy Mansfield Concentration Sidings are almost disused, but household coal is still sent out by rail from collieries at Harworth, Arkwright, Whitwell, Blidworth, Clipstone, Rufford, Mansfield, Ollerton, Calverton, Gedling, Hucknall, Linby, Pye Hill and Rawdon. Only two local coal concentration depots are planned for retention in the entire area, these being at Grimsby (Railway Street) and Lincoln East (Canwick Road).

Another important freight operation is the movement of bulk fuel oil from Immingham's Humber and Lindsey refineries. During a typical working week, about 75 trainloads are dispatched to destinations such as Leeds, Preston, Darwen, Colwick, Brownhills and Bedworth. The quantity of steel traffic conveyed by rail has sadly declined in recent years, but significant tonnages are still carried from the BSC works at Scunthorpe, often in 'Speedlink' trains such as the 6M91 to Bescot, the 6S63 to Aberdeen or the 6V58 to Cardiff. As for the 'Speedlink' operation in general, the chief focal point in the East Midlands is undoubtedly Toton Yard, which dispatches trains to many major centres including Arpley, Bescot, Tyne Yard, Tees Yard, Immingham, Scunthorpe, Harwich, Willesden, Sheerness, Eastleigh and Severn Tunnel Junction. Space here does not permit enumeration of the other freight workings in the area, but full details are given, wherever possible, in the individual photograph captions.

In conclusion, I should like to thank all those who have assisted with the compilation of *Diesels in the East Midlands*. I am particularly grateful to John Cooper-Smith for providing most of the archive material, to Michael Rhodes both for his photographs and for his help and encouragement over the years, and to Rod Nelson for supplying much of the information on signalling.

Paul Shannon
1.12.1985

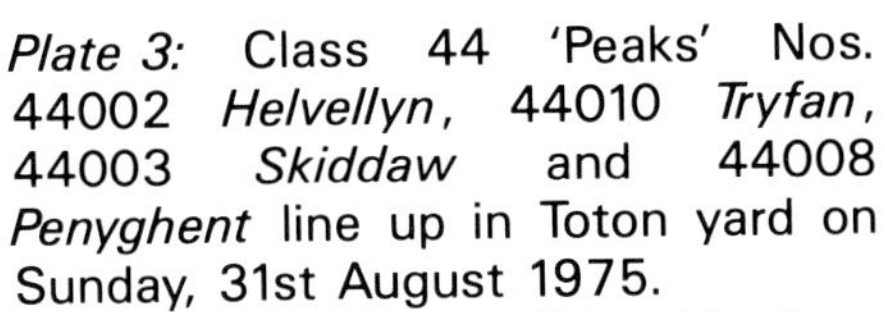

Plate 3: Class 44 'Peaks' Nos. 44002 *Helvellyn*, 44010 *Tryfan*, 44003 *Skiddaw* and 44008 *Penyghent* line up in Toton yard on Sunday, 31st August 1975.

Brian Morrison

South of Leicester

Plate 4: The 08.40 London (St. Pancras) to Nottingham HST accelerates away from Market Harborough on 1st September 1984, with power car No. 43092 leading. The presence of an LNWR signal box at this location is due to the fact that the LNWR line from Northampton was the first to reach the town.

Paul D. Shannon

Plate 5: Midland Railway lower quadrant signals were still very much in evidence at Kibworth when this photograph was taken during July 1967. Green-liveried Class 45/1 'Peak' No. D99 *3rd Carabinier* is seen working a Leeds to London (St. Pancras) express.

J. H. Cooper-Smith

Plate 6: Class 45 'Peak' No. 45143 passes the former station buildings at Great Glen, between Kibworth and Wigston, whilst working the 17.15 London (St. Pancras) to Derby semi-fast service on 3rd July 1983.

Paul D. Shannon

Plate 7: The 14.25 Nottingham to London (St. Pancras) express passes Wigston South Junction on 16th April 1983 in the care of Class 45 'Peak' No. 45146. The lines diverging to the left form a spur to Glen Parva Junction and are occasionally used for diverting passenger trains on to the Midland main line when the West Coast Main Line is blocked south of Nuneaton.

Paul D. Shannon

Leicester

Plate 8: On 16th April 1983, Class 45 No. 45135 approaches Knighton South Junction with the 16.00 semi-fast from Derby to London (St. Pancras). It is here that the freight only line to Coalville diverges.

Paul D. Shannon

Plate 9: An additional Saturday working of 6E69, the 13.30 Langley to Lindsey Oil Refinery empty tank train, is seen approaching Wigston South Junction. Class 47 No. 47292, one of Immingham's allocation, provides the motive power.

Paul D. Shannon

Plate 10: The scrapyard at Braunstone Gate is all that remains of the Great Central Railway in Leicester. On 3rd June 1981, Class 08 No. 08695 shunts MCOs and other wagons, amidst a bewildering arrangement of withdrawn stock.
Paul D. Shannon

Plate 11: Arriving at its destination on 14th April 1984, is the 11.15 from Birmingham (New Street) to Leicester. It is formed of a Class 120 unit comprising cars M53651, M59127 and M53736. Note the impressive station facade, the antiquated signalling and track layout which will soon disappear under the Leicester resignalling scheme.
Paul D. Shannon

Leicester

Plate 12 (left): This view shows Leicester Station as it was in 1974, with Class 45 'Peak' No. D59 arriving with a Sheffield to London (St. Pancras) express. The station roof, dating back to 1890, was finally removed in 1975 to make way for a more modern set of buildings.

J. H. Cooper-Smith

Plate 13 (below left): The 09.00 London (St. Pancras) to Derby HST working arrives at the new Leicester Station on 24th April 1984, with power car 43089 leading.

Paul D. Shannon

Plate 14: Class 31 'Skinhead' No. 31108 heads the 10.20 Birmingham (New Street) to Norwich working past an impressive signal gantry at Bell Lane, north of Leicester, on 30th July 1984.

Paul D. Shannon

Plate 15: Class 31/4 No. 31407 approaches Leicester with the 09.35 Norwich to Birmingham (New Street) working on 24th April 1984. The two tracks immediately to the right of the signal box are used only by freight and light engine movements, with all passenger traffic being concentrated on the left-hand tracks.

Paul D. Shannon

Plate 16: On a dull and drizzly 11th April 1983, Class 56 No. 56049 propels its rake of 35 HAA wagons under the rapid loader at Bagworth Colliery, having arrived as 6F01, the 10.45 empties from Mantle Lane. The Coalville line is famous for its undulating trackwork, which is very evident on the left of this picture.

Paul D. Shannon

Plate 17: Class 47 No. 47229 passes Moira West Junction with a coal train for Drakelow Power-Station on 11th April 1983, as Class 56 No. 56064 edges forward out of Rawdon Colliery Sidings.

Paul D. Shannon

Plate 18 (above right): Since closure of the line to Donisthorpe and Measham from Moira, the sidings at Overseal have been used mainly for empty wagon storage. Here, Class 20 locomotives Nos. 20084 and 20143 depart from Overseal, on 28th July 1983, with a short rake of HTV wagons bound for Cadley Hill Colliery.

Michael Rhodes

Plate 19 (right): A further example of mining subsidence can be seen at Moira West Junction, where Class 56 No. 56064 is taking the Rawdon Colliery branch with its train of empty HAA wagons.

Paul D. Shannon

From Hinckley . . .

Plate 20 (left): Many of the local services between Birmingham and Leicester are worked by Tyseley's Class 116 suburban units. On 14th April 1984, the 09.05 working from Birmingham (New Street) enters Hinckley Station, formed of power cars M51129 and M51142, together with Metropolitan-Cammell trailer car E59101.
Paul D. Shannon

Plate 22 (right): The 08.04 Birmingham (New Street) to Norwich working passes the attractive LMS signal box at Melton Mowbray on 13th April 1984, headed by Class 31/4 locomotive No. 31415.
Paul D. Shannon

Plate 21: Class 31/4 No. 31415 heads the 10.15 Birmingham (New Street) to Norwich working past Croft Sidings, between Hinckley and Narborough.
Paul D. Shannon

. . . towards Stamford

Plate 23: Class 45 'Peak' No. 45003 heads westwards through Frisby, on 30th July 1984, with a local trip working from Melton Mowbray. The two Interfrigo ferry vans are used to carry pet food for a local factory.

Paul D. Shannon

Plate 24: The trackwork at Melton Mowbray has remained essentially unchanged for decades, and thus provides plenty of interest for the modeller. On 7th January 1982, Class 40 No. 40077 accelerates away with 6E43, the 14.05 Corby to Lackenby steel coil empties, consisting of eleven BBA wagons.

Paul D. Shannon

Plate 25: On 13th April 1984, Class 20 locomotives Nos. 20161 and 20168 pass through Melton Mowbray Station on their way from Toton Depot to Corby BSC sidings.

Paul D. Shannon

Plate 26: The 14.05 Birmingham (New Street) to Peterborough train speeds through Frisby on 15th April 1984, and is worked by a Swindon-built Class 120 unit. Signal boxes such as Frisby (and Whissendine in *Plate 27*) have survived mainly because they control level crossings.

Paul D. Shannon

Plate 27: Class 47 No. 47102 passes the Midland Railway signal box at Whissendine on 30th July 1984, heading 7E98, the 14.29 Mountsorrel to Hitchin engineer's ballast train.

Paul D. Shannon

Plate 28 (left): Class 20 locomotives Nos. 20168 and 20161 head northwards past Manton Junction with a special working of tube wagons from Corby to Toton on 13th April 1984. The track layout and arrangement of colour light signals both show how the Corby line was once considered to be the more important route, whereas most trains nowadays use the Peterborough-bound tracks, seen to the left of the picture.

Paul D. Shannon

Plate 30 (right): Class 25 No. 25194 approaches Stamford with 6M44, the 11.21 Ketton to Castle Bromwich cement train, conveying its load in yellow-liveried PCA wagons. Because of the track layout at Ketton, this train has to run eastwards as far as Peterborough, where it reverses and heads back along the Leicester line, passing its originating point for the second time about an hour after departure!

Paul D. Shannon

Plate 31 (below right): The use of a 200mm. lens compresses Stamford's railway and non-railway architecture alike, as Class 31/4 No. 31421 departs with the 09.35 Norwich to Birmingham (New Street) service on 13th April 1984.

Paul D. Shannon

Plate 29 (below): Manton Junction box was switched out on Sunday, 3rd July 1983, when Class 31/4 No. 31412 was photographed hauling the 15.52 Cambridge to Birmingham (New Street) working. Notice the short wooden-posted signal of Midland Railway origin in the centre of the picture.

Paul D. Shannon

Leicester to Trent

Plate 32: The 12.35 Sheffield to London (St. Pancras) working passes the Blue Circle Cement Terminal at Syston South Junction on 16th April 1983. The sidings here are served by a weekly block train from Earle's Sidings, running overnight in both directions.

Rod Nelson

Plate 34 (right): On the evening of 27th June 1983, Class 47 locomotive, No. 47328, is pictured approaching Loughborough Station with a northbound 'Speedlink' working. The single line, which diverges in the middle distance, forms a spur to the former Great Central line to East Leake and Ruddington, and was constructed in 1974 to permit closure of the section between Ruddington and Nottingham (Victoria).

Michael Rhodes

Plate 35 (below right): Class 45 'Peak' No. 45141 speeds past Sileby on 16th April 1983 with the 12.19 Derby to London (St. Pancras) express.

Paul D. Shannon

Plate 33: Only a few weeks before all vacuum-braked wagonload traffic was officially discontinued on British Rail, Class 45 'Peak' No. 45063 approaches Sileby with 9M75, the 10.20 Temple Mills to Toton (New Bank) working on 13th April 1984. The only loaded wagons are MXVs, with scrap metal bound for South Yorkshire.

Paul D. Shannon

Plate 36 (left): Rather unceremoniously, HSTs took over the bulk of Midland main line services in May 1983. Here, the 15.45 London (St. Pancras) to Nottingham service is seen at Barrow-on-Soar on 13th April 1984, with power car No. 43154 leading.

Paul D. Shannon

Plate 38 (right): The 13.55 Derby to London (St. Pancras) HST enters Loughborough Station on 14th April 1984, with power car No. 43057 *Bounds Green* leading. The sidings on the left are normally used for marshalling engineer's ballast trains, but were out of use on this date as the former goods shed was being demolished.

Paul D. Shannon

Plate 37 (below): One of the oldest Class 25s still in service, No. 25044, heads 7E59, the 16.12 Colwick Estate to Ripple Lane empty tank train, through Barrow-on-Soar.

Paul D. Shannon

LOUCHBORO'
43057

58004

Plate 40: Ratcliffe's giant cooling towers dominate the scene as a three car Class 120 diesel multiple unit heads north with the 17.29 Leicester to Derby service.

Paul D. Shannon

Plate 39 (left): Class 58 No. 58004 edges forward out of the power-station sidings at Ratcliffe on the evening of 24th April 1984. It will now return to Toton Yard where the wagons will be stabled until the next morning.

Paul D. Shannon

Plate 41 (right): A Class 47 locomotive, No. 47314, passes Ratcliffe with 6E69, the 13.30 Langley to Humber Oil Refinery empty tank train.

Paul D. Shannon

Via Castle Donington

Plate 42: The line from Stenson Junction to Trent is rather busier than a first glance might suggest. In addition to local merry-go-round trains to Castle Donington and Willington power-stations, a number of 'Speedlink' and other freight workings from Toton to the West Midlands are sent this way. This picture shows Class 20 locomotives Nos. 20167 and 20161 heading east, near Castle Donington, on 27th July 1984.

Paul D. Shannon

Plate 44 (right): Class 25 locomotives Nos. 25302 and 25285 rejoin the main line at Willington on 2nd August 1984 with 8E36, the thrice weekly 18.10 Longport Junction to Worksop sand train. This train is one of a handful which travel via Uttoxeter, and conveys sand, in HJV and HKV wagons from Oakamoor BIS siding, to be used in the manufacturing of glass.

Paul D. Shannon

Plate 43 (below): With the cooling towers of Castle Donington Power-Station looming glumly in the background, Class 56 No. 56083 approaches Weston-on-Trent with a westbound ballast train on the evening of 2nd August 1984.

Paul D. Shannon

Plate 45: A Class 120/101 unit, comprising cars M53713, E59524 and M53667, draws into Uttoxeter Station on 10th April 1984, whilst working the 09.20 Crewe to Lincoln (St. Mark's) service.

Paul D. Shannon

Plate 46: This is what the south end of Derby Station looked like in August 1966. The intricate trackwork, the semaphore signalling, including some lower quadrants, and even the pre-nationalisation goods vans are all features of a past era, as are, of course, the green liveried locomotive and maroon coaches. The train is a Bristol to Newcastle express, headed by Class 47 No. D1989.

J. H. Cooper-Smith

Plate 47: Newly-overhauled and newly-named Class 45 'Peak', No. D99 *3rd Carabinier* awaits departure from Derby with the 20.00 working to London (St. Pancras) on 8th January 1966.

J. H. Cooper-Smith

Derby

Plate 48 (above right): Class 08 shunter No. 08178 stands at Derby Station on 22nd November 1975. Notice the ex-GWR Toad brake van in the sidings to the right of the picture.

Brian Morrison

Plate 49 (right): Although the main running lines are controlled from Derby power box, the mechanical signal box at Spondon is retained for shunting movements to and from the CEGB and British Celanese private sidings. Here, the 10.30 London (St. Pancras) to Sheffield HST working is seen heading towards Derby on 3rd August 1984.

Paul D. Shannon

Derby
08 178
adidas

Plate 50: Class 56 No. 56010 passes Melbourne Junction, near Peartree, with an 'up' merry-go-round train on 1st July 1983.

Brian Morrison

Plate 52 (right): Class 31 locomotives have taken over many duties which were formerly the preserve of Classes 20 and 25. On 15th April 1983, Class 31 No. 31293 departs from the sidings at Wirksworth with a trip freight to Derby (St. Mary's) conveying limestone in four MSV wagons.

Paul D. Shannon

Plate 53 (below right): The 09.15 Matlock to Derby service pulls out of Matlock Bath Station on 24th July 1984, and is worked by a four car Class 120/101 diesel multiple unit. The station here was closed at the same time as the through route from Matlock to Buxton, but it was reopened in May 1972, and has since been a great success.

Paul D. Shannon

Plate 51: The line to Sinfin (Central) was reopened to passenger traffic on 4th October 1976, but loadings were poor, and the service was cut back to a bare minimum only three months later. Here, a Swindon Class 120 diesel multiple unit leaves Sinfin (Central) with the 08.01 service to Derby and Matlock, this being one of the three daily departures.

Brian Morrison

CAFE

Derby to Clay Cross

Plate 54 (left): In blue livery but with its headcode panel still in use, a Class 45 'Peak' locomotive heads a Sheffield to London (St. Pancras) express towards Duffield, in October 1973.

J. H. Cooper-Smith

Plate 56 (right): Since the May 1984 timetable change, locomotive-hauled trains have once again become a more common sight on North-East to South-West services. On 1st September 1984, the 09.22 Newcastle to Penzance working enjoyed 'Peak' haulage, and is seen near the former station of Wingfield.

Paul D. Shannon

Plate 57 (below right): Class 25 No. 5164 emerges from Ambergate Tunnel with an 'up' train of FVV Carflats in September 1971.

J. H. Cooper-Smith

Plate 55 (below): The 10.35 Matlock to Derby working heads south along the main line near Ambergate on 15th April 1983, and is formed of diesel multiple unit cars M53704, M59089 and M53676.

Paul D. Shannon

4M38

Toton

Plate 58: Class 45 No. 45064 threads its way out of Toton East Yard with 8V26, the 15.51 to Acton, on 3rd June 1981. This train was conveying coal for a large variety of destinations in the south-east, including Luton and Neasden coal concentration depots.

Paul D. Shannon

Plate 59: On 10th July 1984, Class 25 No. 25257 arrives at Toton North Yard with a trip freight from the south. The sidings here present a sadly desolate appearance, with nothing but rakes of coal wagons, immobilised due to the miners' strike.

Michael Rhodes

Plate 60: Class 37 No. 37290 heads north past Stapleford & Sandiacre signal box on 3rd June 1981 with 6E12, the 17.45 Spondon to Saltend chemicals train.

Paul D. Shannon

Plate 61: Super power is provided for 6M47, the 10.45 Lackenby to Corby steel coil train, in the shape of Class 56 locomotives Nos. 56101 and 56009, seen heading south at Toton on 9th July 1984.

Michael Rhodes

Nottingham

Plate 62: Class 20 locomotives Nos. 20198 and 20199 head a train of empty HUO wagons through Nottingham Station on 10th July 1984, bound for the nearby Gedling Colliery. The Gedling to Spondon circuit was the last regular operation with unfitted wagons on the London Midland Region, continuing long after other power-stations in the area had been converted to merry-go-round operation.

Michael Rhodes

Plate 63: The station facade and former goods warehouse at Nottingham provide a contrast with British Rail's Inter-City image, as HST power car No. 43089 leads the 15.00 departure to London (St. Pancras) out of the station on 3rd August 1984.

Paul D. Shannon

Plate 64: Class 40 No. 40194 passes Beeston Freightliner Depot with a train of track sections, bound for Rugby, on 3rd August 1984. All of Nottingham's wagonload traffic is now marshalled in the few sidings between the Freightliner Depot and the main lines, seen in this picture.

Paul D. Shannon

Plate 65: The Midland Railway box at Sneinton, just east of Nottingham, is retained to control the level crossing there. On 27th July 1984, a Swindon Class 120 unit is seen forming the 09.07 Birmingham (New Street) to Lincoln (St. Mark's) stopping train.

Paul D. Shannon

10
42
D6754

Plate 68: Class 20 locomotives Nos. 20147 and 20183 pass Lincoln Street Crossing, the junction for the now-closed Babbington branch, with a train of household coal from Bestwood Park to Toton on 14th April 1983.

Paul D. Shannon

Plate 69: The modern NCB installations at Hucknall Colliery form a contrast with the Midland Railway signal box and semaphore signals, as Class 47 No. 47364 heads south with a rake of 43 HAA wagons destined for Ratcliffe Power-Station.

Paul D. Shannon

Plates 66 & 67 (left): Two nostalgic views of the long-closed Victoria Station on the former Great Central main line through Nottingham. Class 37, No. D6813 (*top picture*) pauses with an evening through train from Bournemouth to York in January 1965, whilst the lower picture shows Class 37 No D6754 passing the unique signal box at the north end of the station, with a York to Bournemouth express, in June of the same year.

J. H. Cooper-Smith

Plate 70: Class 47 No. 47195 passes Bestwood Park Sidings with the 6T54 Newstead to Ratcliffe merry-go-round train on 14th April 1983.

Paul D. Shannon

Plate 71: The Newstead branch is now closed beyond Linby Colliery, but a few months before its closure, Class 47 No. 47364 was photographed arriving at the end of the branch with the 6T53 empties from Ratcliffe Power-Station, ready for reloading and yet another run on the merry-go-round circuit.

Paul D. Shannon

Plate 72: On 10th July 1984, Class 58 No. 58008 passes through Ilkeston North with empty HAA wagons from Ratcliffe to Tibshelf Sidings.
Michael Rhodes

Plate 73: Class 45 No. 45017 heads 7E42, the 16.54 Toton to Dringhouses 'Speedlink' working past Trowell Junction on 10th July 1984. The first two wagons are examples of the new POA scrap metal carriers, built to replace British Rail's ageing MCV and MXV types. The line diverging to the left leads to Nottingham, and has recently been proposed for singling, or maybe even complete closure.
Michael Rhodes

Plate 74: Class 20 locomotives Nos. 20135 and 20195 head 8M04, the 08.29 Mansfield to Toton coal train past Bennerley Junction on 14th April 1983. The train is composed entirely of vacuum-braked HTV hoppers, and so would have been running as a Class 6 freight on this date.

Paul D. Shannon

Plate 75: During 1983/4, a new rapid coal loader was constructed at Bennerley Opencast Disposal Site, overshadowing the well-known Great Northern Railway viaduct which crosses the Erewash Valley at this point. Here, the 16.00 Sheffield to London (St. Pancras) working is headed by HST power car No. 43103, on 31st July 1984.

Paul D. Shannon

Plate 76: Alfreton & Mansfield Parkway Station was opened on 7th May 1973, seven years after a local station on the same site (but named Alfreton & South Normanton) had been closed. In addition to London-bound HST workings, the station is now served by all three pairs of services on the Nottingham to Manchester route, and this picture shows Class 47 No. 47433 arriving with the 10.09 Barrow-in-Furness to Nottingham working on 24th July 1984.

Paul D. Shannon

Plate 77: Class 20 locomotives Nos. 20190 and 20173 are seen at Westhouses on 21st May 1983, just a few months before the former steam depot here was finally closed. Locomotives are now stabled in the sidings at Tibshelf, adjacent to the main line.

Paul D. Shannon

. . . and on to Chesterfield

Plate 78: Class 40 No. 40152 approaches Do
Hill, north of Tibshelf, with a 'down' ballast trai
on the evening of 14th April 1983.
Paul D. Shanno

Plate 79: Class 56 No. 56048 passes an interesting set of signals, as it leaves Tibshelf Sidings with the 6T03 Sutton to Willington Power-Station merry-go-round working on 12th March 1982.
Michael Rhodes

Plate 80: Approaching Clay Cross on 21st May 1983, is the 10.16 Barrow-in-Furness to Nottingham service, headed by Class 47 No. 47491.

Paul D. Shannon

Plate 81: Privately-owned engines *Avenue 4* (right) and *Avenue 7* (left), shunt, on 9th September 1983, at Avenue Sidings, between Chesterfield and Clay Cross. These were exchange sidings for traffic into and out of the Avenue Coking Plant, but were closed and lifted shortly after this photograph was taken. British Rail merry-go-round trains now run directly into the plant.

Stewart Jolly

Plate 82 (left): Class 40 No. 40050 pauses at Chesterfield with the 18.09 Manchester (Piccadilly) to London (St. Pancras) parcels train on 29th December 1982.

Stewart Jolly

Plate 84 (right): Cravens diesel multiple unit cars E51299 and E54424 form the 17.31 Sheffield to New Mills (Central) stopping train, and are seen approaching Bamford on 4th July 1983.

Paul D. Shannon

Plate 83: Trains pass north of Chesterfield on 19th September 1981. The 12.10 Sheffield to London (St. Pancras working is headed by Class 45 No. 45120, and the northbound empty Freightliner flats are drawn by Class 47 No. 47053.

Michael J. Collins

BAMFORD

Plate 85 (left): Permanent way staff pause for a few moments, as a New Mills to Sheffield local train approaches Edale on 26th March 1981. Notice the mixed appearance of the Class 114 unit; E56019 was still in all-over blue, whereas E50003 had recently been painted in the new standard livery of blue and grey.

Paul D. Shannon

Plate 86 (right): Class 40 No. 40015 heads the afternoon Cleethorpes to Manchester newspaper empties through Edale on 5th July 1983.

Paul D. Shannon

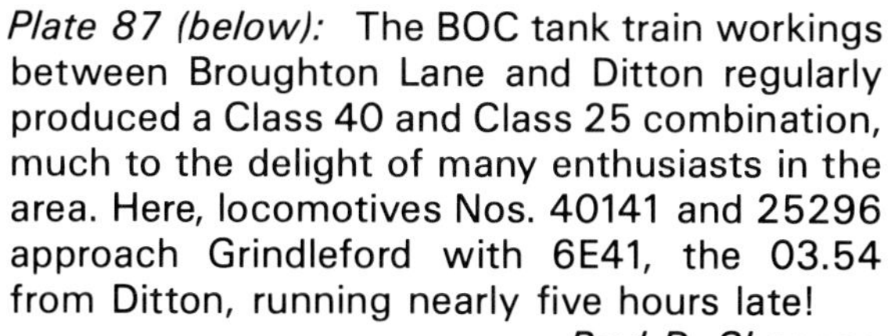

Plate 87 (below): The BOC tank train workings between Broughton Lane and Ditton regularly produced a Class 40 and Class 25 combination, much to the delight of many enthusiasts in the area. Here, locomotives Nos. 40141 and 25296 approach Grindleford with 6E41, the 03.54 from Ditton, running nearly five hours late!

Paul D. Shannon

Plate 88: Until May 1984, most main line services via the Hope Valley were operated by Class 123/124 diesel multiple units. Here, the 09.15 Manchester (Piccadilly) to Hull train is formed by cars E52088, E59773, E59819 and E52097, as it passes Totley Tunnel East box on 5th July 1983.

Paul D. Shannon

Plate 89: Class 47 No. 47480 *Robin Hood* heads the 10.16 Barrow-in-Furness to Nottingham working towards Bamford on 26th April 1984.

John Hillmer

Plate 90: Barrow Hill boasted a veritable forest of semaphore signals until the area was taken over by Sheffield power box in the autumn of 1981. Here, Class 45 No. 45057 passes Barrow Hill Junction box with 6M77, the 10.45 York to Loughborough empty ballast train.

Paul D. Shannon

Plate 91: Class 20 locomotives Nos. 20142 and 20183 head north through Barrow Hill on 27th July 1981 with 8E16, the 09.30 Bescot to Tinsley freight. Notice the delightful assortment of wagons on this service — STV, MCV, UCV, BPV, BCV, VIX, VVV, HTV and KTV types are all represented!

Paul D. Shannon

Plate 92: The only passenger trains to pass through Barrow Hill in 1981 were diversions and excursions, such as this one in the care of Class 47 No. 47210. Nowadays, however, the Barrow-in-Furness to Nottingham service is scheduled to run this way, in order to avoid reversal at Sheffield, and until the summer of 1983, the two services to and from Glasgow did the same.

Paul D. Shannon

Plate 93: Grouped around the turntable in Barrow Hill engine shed are Nos. 20132, 47307, 08267, 20007 and 47281. The photograph was taken in January 1977, before the new build of Class 56 locomotives had started to make an impact in the area.

Michael Rhodes

Plate 94: Class 45 No. 45068 passes Foxlow Junction with 4M33, the 12.20 Wrenthorpe to Bescot car train, on 27th July 1981.

Paul D. Shannon

Plate 95 (left): Single Class 20 locomotives at work are a common sight in the Barrow Hill area. Here, No. 20211 approaches Markham Colliery Sidings with the 9T94 empties from Bolsover Coalite to Barrow Hill, consisting entirely of unfitted MCO wagons.

Paul D. Shannon

Plate 96 (right): On 15th June 1981, a Class 56 locomotive, No. 56010, negotiates the pointwork at Markam Colliery Sidings with the 6T86 merry-go-round empties from Barrow Hill. The train will run forward as 6V51 to Didcot Power-Station.

Paul D. Shannon

Plate 97: Class 20 No. 20064 heads a Bolsover to Barrow Hill coal train past Seymour Junction on the evening of 27th July 1981. Notice the abundance of semaphore signals in the yard, all of which have now disappeared.

Paul D. Shannon

Shirebrook

Plate 98: On 28th August 1979, a Class 56 locomotive, No. 56007, heads a loaded merry-go-round train south of Shirebrook.
Les Nixon

Plate 99: On 26th August 1983, the 17.30 Worksop to Toton 'Speedlink' train (6M70) passes the south end of Shirebrook Depot in the care of Class 31 No. 31227.
Les Nixon

Plate 100: Locomotives of Classes 56, 37 and 20 are stabled at Shirebrook Depot on 21st May 1983. Those nearest the camera are Nos. 56098 and 56117.

Paul D. Shannon

Plate 101: Class 56 No. 56002 propels its train of empty HAA wagons on to the 'up' line at Shirebrook on 15th June 1981, before proceeding along the single track to Warsop Main Colliery.

Paul D. Shannon

Around Mansfield

Plate 102: On 24th July 1984, Class 56 No. 56021 arrives at Mansfield Concentration Sidings with the 6Z76 merry-go-round empties from Ratcliffe Power-Station. These sidings now see little use apart from wagon storage, since virtually all traffic is now handled in block trains.

Paul D. Shannon

Plate 103: Class 37 No. 37215 passes Clipstone West Junction on 12th April 1984, with an engineer's special train returning from track lifting duties at High Marnham. The spur to the right of the picture leads to Mansfield Concentration Sidings.

Paul D. Shannon

Plate 104: An extraordinary relic which survived into the 1980s was this collection of Midland Railway lower quadrant signals at Rufford Colliery Sidings. On 14th April 1977, Class 20 locomotives Nos. 20134 and 20136 approach the junction with a partially-fitted coal train from Clipstone. The line from Mansfield South Junction to Rufford was closed completely on 12th December 1983, and all traffic to the London Midland Region is now diverted via Shirebrook.

Les Nixon

The High Marnham Branch

Plate 105: Class 20 locomotives Nos. 20010 and 20056 pass Welbec
Colliery Junction with a short eastbound trip freight on 15th April 1983.

Paul D. Shanno

Plate 106: A new private siding was built for the Butterley Brickworks at Kirton during 1984. Running as Mansfield 'target 02', Class 37 No. 37209 has just run round its train of empty OCA and OBA wagons in the loop at Boughton Junction, and will now propel it down the main line as far as the works.

Paul D. Shannon

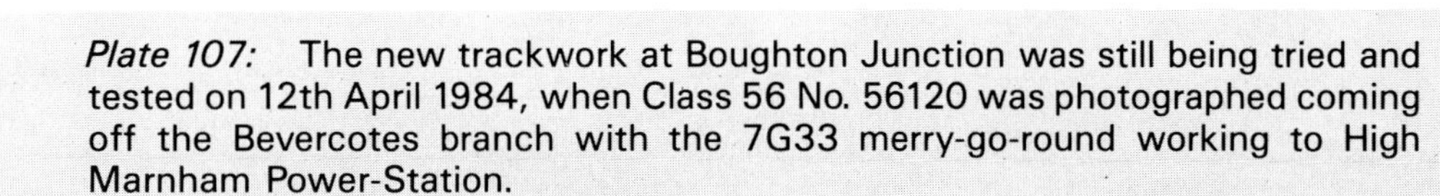

Plate 107: The new trackwork at Boughton Junction was still being tried and tested on 12th April 1984, when Class 56 No. 56120 was photographed coming off the Bevercotes branch with the 7G33 merry-go-round working to High Marnham Power-Station.

Paul D. Shannon

Plate 108: Class 31 No. 31302 passes the Great Central signal box at Ollerton Colliery on 15th June 1981, with the 8T19 local trip freight from Ollerton to Mansfield Concentration Sidings.

Paul D. Shannon

Plate 109: Despite the miners' strike, High Marnham Power-Station was receiving more than its usual quota of coal trains during April 1984, as the unloading facilities at both West Burton and Cottam power-stations were out of order. Here, Class 56 No. 56117 arrives at High Marnham with the 7G34 merry-go-round working from Ollerton.

Paul D. Shannon

Shirebrook to Worksop

Plate 110: Class 56 No. 56085 heads south through the site of the former station of Whitwell with the 6F61 empties from Cottam Power-Station on 15th April 1983.
Paul D. Shannon

Plate 111: The 6T61 trip working to Worksop is seen leaving Whitwell Colliery Sidings on 15th April 1983, hauled by Class 20 locomotives Nos. 20008 and 20026, and conveying four HTV wagons laden with coal for Grimsby.
Paul D. Shannon

Plate 112 (right): Class 56 No. 56015 heads south through Elmton & Creswell with the standard load of 34 empty HAA wagons on 15th April 1983. Elmton signal box has been retained to control the junction with the little-used branch to Seymour and Barrow Hill.
Paul D. Shannon

Plate 113 (below): Coal for export via Garston Docks is generally conveyed in HBA type hopper wagons. Here, Class 37 locomotives Nos. 37174 and 37226 emerge from Whitwell Tunnel with 6M20, the 11.52 Ollerton to Garston working, on 15th April 1983.
Paul D. Shannon

Plate 114 (above right): Class 20 locomotives Nos. 20208 and 20133 depart from Harworth Colliery Sidings with the 6T64 local trip freight to Worksop, conveying domestic coal in MCV wagons. Notice also the presence of HAA and HBA type wagons in the sidings.
Paul D. Shannon

Plate 115 (right): A triangle of lines remained in use at Firbeck until June 1983, when the area was resignalled and the spur from East Junction to South Junction was closed. On 13th April 1983, Class 20 locomotives Nos. 20015 and 20154 take the Harworth line at Firbeck West Junction with the 6T68 merry-go-round empties to West Burton.
Paul D. Shannon

The Harworth Branch

SHEFFIELD
Worksop
West

Plate 118 (right): Class 56 No. 56099 accelerates away from West Burton Power-Station with a westbound train of empty HAA wagons on the evening of 15th April 1983.

Paul D. Shannon

Plate 116 (left): The signal box at Worksop West is one of the oldest on British Rail, being of Manchester, Sheffield & Lincolnshire Railway origin. Here, the 17.28 Retford to Sheffield train is worked by a Class 101 unit, comprising cars E54383 and E53217, on 24th July 1984.

Paul D. Shannon

Plate 117 (below left): One of the steady stream of merry-go-round trains from West Burton and Cottam power-stations is seen approaching Whisker Hill Junction, near Retford, on 15th July 1983. The locomotive in charge is Class 56 No. 56097.

Paul D. Shannon

Plate 119 (below): The 16.12 Retford to Sheffield service passes Shireoaks East Junction on 24th July 1984, and is worked by a Class 114 unit, comprising cars E54016 and E53032.

Paul D. Shannon

The East Coast Main Line

Plate 120 (above): Six months before the last member of the class was withdrawn from service, Class 55 'Deltic' No. 55009 *Alycidon* pauses at Grantham with the 18.05 London (King's Cross) to York semi-fast working, on 3rd June 1981.

Paul D. Shannon

Plate 122 (above right): In 1966, the place of the 'Deltics' as top rank express locomotives must have seemed irrefutable. On 18th August of that year, green-liveried Class 55 'Deltic' No. D9019 *Royal Highland Fusilier* was photographed heading the 'up' 'Flying Scotsman' at Little Ponton.

J. H. Cooper-Smith

Plate 123 (right): After most East Coast Main Line expresses had been taken over by HSTs, the remaining 'Deltics' were left to work semi-fast trains between London (King's Cross) and York. Here, Class 55 'Deltic' No. 55017 *The Durham Light Infantry* approaches Helpston with a northbound service, on the evening of 1st August 1981.

Paul D. Shannon

Plate 121 (left): Class 55 'Deltic' No. D9016 *Gordon Highlander* races past Essendine, on 30th May 1966, with the 12.00 Edinburgh to London (King's Cross) express.

J. H. Cooper-Smith

1A35

Plate 124 (above): Freight trains on the East Coast Main Line are generally few and far between, but on weekday evenings there are three 'down' 'Speedlink' services, which often run within the space of an hour or so. The first of these is 6S96, the 13.50 Parkeston Yard to Mossend working, seen here at Great Ponton behind Class 37 No. 37084.

Paul D. Shannon

Plate 126 (above right): Newly overhauled Class 37 No. 37147 heads north near Sutton-on-Trent with an evening 'Speedlink' service on 31st July 1984. The two Campbell's Soups vans have come from King's Lynn, and have tarpaulined sides to facilitate loading by fork-lift truck.

Paul D. Shannon

Plate 127 (right): The 18.21 Whitemoor to Mossend 'Speedlink' working (6S71) approaches Grantham on 25th July 1984, headed by Class 47 No. 47231. Amongst the loads carried are several tanks of molasses from Peterborough to the Distillers factory at Menstrie, near Stirling.

Paul D. Shannon

Plate 125 (left): Class 47 No. 47303 has just emerged from Peascliffe Tunnel with 6B61, the 11.10 Sleaford to Peterborough trip freight which, on 31st July 1984, consisted of two empty UKF fertiliser vans (PWA) on their way back to Ince & Elton.

Paul D. Shannon

Campbell's Soups Limited
D
20

Plate 128: Regular 125m.p.h. running was introduced on the East Coast Main Line in May 1978. In this scene, HST power car No. 43156 leads the 17.00 London (King's Cross) to Glasgow (Queen Street) train round the curve at Tuxford, shortly before passing under the High Marnham branch.

Paul D. Shannon

Plate 129: The 12.50 Doncaster to London (King's Cross) semi-fast working passes the modern crossing box at Barnby, just south of Newark, on 31st July 1984. The leading power car is No. 43062.

Paul D. Shannon

Plate 130: The 11.32 Nottingham to Grantham train approaches Bingham on 16th April 1983, and is worked by Class 114 unit E53046 and E54036.

Paul D. Shannon

Plate 131: On 30th July 1984, the 15.40 Skegness to Nottingham train passes an impressive lattice post bracket signal as it enters Bingham Station from the east.

Paul D. Shannon

Plate 132: A South Yorkshire PTE-liveried Class 114 unit, comprising cars E53045 and E54004, approaches Bottesford West Junction with the 10.40 Nottingham to Skegness service on 26th July 1984.

Paul D. Shannon

Plate 133: Class 46 'Peak' No. 46026 *Leicestershire and Derbyshire Yeomanry* passes through Aslockton Station with an eastbound excursion on 16th April 1983.

Paul D. Shannon

Plate 134: The line from Bottesford to Newark sees little use, apart from oil trains to Colwick or Rectory Junction. On 31st July 1984, Class 56 No. 56085 passes the only signal box on the line, at Lowfield, with 7E38, the 09.54 Rectory Junction to Lindsey Oil Refinery empties.

Paul D. Shannon

Plate 135: Class 56 No. 56009 waits at the Rectory Junction Oil Terminal on 3rd August 1984, whilst its tank train is being discharged. It will return north as the 7E38 to Lindsey Oil Refinery.

Paul D. Shannon

Grantham to Skegness

Plate 138 (right): Class 31 No. 31312 passes a somersault shunting signal at the west end of Sleaford Yard, as it arrives with the 08.15 Leeds to Yarmouth holiday train.

Paul D. Shannon

Plate 139 (below right): On 31st July 1984, Class 31 No. 31161 keeps pedestrians waiting at the east end of Sleaford Station, as it prepares to depart with the 08.46 Sheffield to Skegness train.

Paul D. Shannon

Plate 136: The line from Barkston to Allington is used only by summer Saturday trains to Skegness and the occasional special freight from Boston Docks. On 16th July 1983, Class 45 No. 45007 approaches Barkston East Junction with the 07.32 Sheffield to Skegness working.

Paul D. Shannon

Plate 137: The use of Class 20 locomotives on Skegness holiday trains has attracted a great number of 'haulage' enthusiasts to the area. Here, Nos. 20183 and 20187 head the 08.38 working from Leicester through Ancaster on 16th July 1983.

Paul D. Shannon

SLEAFORD WEST
20

Sleaford
East
15

Plate 140: A 28mm. lens was used to capture this view of the famous Heckington windmill. Class 20 locomotives, Nos. 20160 and 20140 are heading the 08.48 Leicester to Skegness holiday train on Tuesday, 31st July 1984.

Paul D. Shannon

Plate 141: A rather unusual BR-built signal box controls the level crossing at Hubberts Bridge, where Class 37 No. 37196 is seen with the 08.04 Manchester (Piccadilly) to Skegness working on 16th July 1983.

Paul D. Shannon

Plate 142: Class 47 No. 47026 draws into Boston Station with the 15.35 Skegness to Peterborough train on 16th July 1983. Flower beds now occupy the space where, in more prosperous days, there would have been two 'through roads'.

Paul D. Shannon

Plate 143: Class 31 No. 31190 has just arrived at Boston with the 9T21 trip working from Lincoln, on 31st July 1984. It will now set back into the goods yard, where Class 08 No. 08386 will position the two Polybulk grain wagons ready for loading by conveyor belt.

Paul D. Shannon

Wainfleet

Plate 146: Two lower quadrant somersault signals of Great Northern Railway origin survive at Havenhouse, where Class 31 No. 31272 is seen with the 13.37 Skegness to Leeds holiday train on 1st August 1981.

Paul D. Shannon

Plate 144 (top left): On 1st August 1981, Class 40 No. 40013 rounds the bend at Wainfleet whilst heading the 13.19 service from Skegness to Manchester (Piccadilly).

Paul D. Shannon

Plate 145 (left): Class 31 No. 31410 approaches Wainfleet with the 14.36 Skegness to Leeds working on 16th July 1983.

Paul D. Shannon

Plate 147 (right): Class 20 locomotives Nos. 20143 and 20150 propel the stock of the 08.16 from Leicester into the carriage sidings at Skegness on 18th August 1984.

Kim Fullbrook

Plate 149: The direct line between March and Spalding was closed in November 1982, with all traffic being diverted via Peterborough. Class 25 locomotives Nos. 25032 and 25286 are seen passing through Cowbit on 20th June 1981 with the 14.20 Yarmouth to Derby holiday train.

Paul D. Shannon

Plate 148 (left): Once a year, the normally quiet station at Spalding becomes a hive of activity, with a large number of special trains for the famous 'Flower Parade Day'. In 1982, excursions operated from Newcastle upon Tyne, Swindon, Weston-super-Mare, New Mills (Central), Guildford, West Ruislip, Swansea, Plymouth, Liverpool, Tonbridge, Wellington and Bicester. Class 47 No. 47533 is pictured here arriving with the 1Z39 special from Swindon, whilst Class 46 'Peak' No. 46047 shunts the stock of the 1G31 excursion from Newcastle upon Tyne.

Paul D. Shannon

Plate 150 (right): Class 20 locomotives Nos. 20142 and 20113 head 8E57, the 09.52 Wirksworth to Whitemoor freight, through Spalding on 8th October 1980. This train ran only during the sugar beet season, and conveyed limestone in unfitted HUO hopper wagons to several East Anglian sugar factories.

Michael Rhodes

Plate 151 (below): The 12.38 Doncaster to Cambridge train pulls out of Spalding Station on 8th May 1982, and is worked by a Cravens Class 105 unit, comprising cars E56133 and E51270.

Paul D. Shannon

The Joint Line

Plate 152 (above): The 'Joint' line between Spalding and Doncaster has survived partly because of its usefulness as a diversionary route for the East Coast Main Line. On 2nd February 1982, a landslip near Grantham caused such diversions to take place, and a southbound HST is seen approaching Helpringham.

Rod Nelson

Plate 153 (below): By July 1983, Helpringham signal box had been closed, and the structure reduced to an empty shell. Class 40 No. 40129 heads north with the 14.34 Yarmouth to Manchester (Piccadilly) summer Saturday train.

Paul D. Shannon

Plate 154: The thirteen coach 08.35 Newcastle to Yarmouth train approaches Sleaford North Junction, on 20th June 1981, hauled by Class 40 No. 40049.
Paul D. Shannon

Plate 155: Class 40 No. 40136 passes Sleaford North Junction with the 09.20 Yarmouth to Newcastle service on 20th June 1981. The single track to the right leads round into Sleaford Station, whilst the train pictured here is just coming off the threatened avoiding line.
Paul D. Shannon

Plate 156: Ruskington Station was reopened in May 1975, after fourteen years of closure. Class 31 No. 31253 is seen here approaching the station with the 09.10 Leeds to Yarmouth service.

Paul D. Shannon

Plate 157: Class 47 No. 47372 heads south through Metheringham (formerly Blankney & Metheringham) with the 08.40 Chesterfield to Skegness working on 20th June 1981.

Paul D. Shannon

Plate 158: The 08.58 Boston to Doncaster train passes through Potterhanworth on 16th April 1983, formed by one of Lincoln's well-travelled Class 114 diesel multiple units.

Paul D. Shannon

Nottingham to Lincoln

Plate 159: Lowdham is a delightful location for any signalling enthusiast, as it retains both wheel-operated level crossing gates and a lattice post repeater signal. On 30th July 1984, the 15.20 Crewe to Lincoln (St. Mark's) train pulls away from the station, and comprises diesel multiple unit cars M53670, M59524 and M53744.

Paul D. Shannon

Plate 160: A two-hourly through service between Lincoln and Crewe was introduced in May 1973, operated then, as today, by Swindon cross-country diesel multiple units. Here, the 18.45 from Lincoln (St. Mark's) is seen passing Staythorpe Crossing box, on 26th July 1984.

Paul D. Shannon

Plate 161: The 15.40 Lincoln (St. Mark's) to Crewe train draws to a halt at Newark Castle Station, and is worked by a Class 120 unit, comprising cars M53656, M59531 and M53743.

Paul D. Shannon

Plate 162: Class 31 No. 31291 heads 7Z15, the 10.41 Immingham to Brierley Hill Steel Terminal working through Swinderby on 26th July 1984, conveying steel coil loaded on to BEV and JTV wagons.

Paul D. Shannon

Plate 163: Class 31/4 No. 31409 arrives at Lincoln (St. Mark's) with the 09.45 Newark (North Gate) to Cleethorpes train on 13th April 1983. Construction of the new spur to Boultham Junction will allow closure of Lincoln (St. Mark's) Station, and concentrate all rail traffic over the one level crossing adjacent to Lincoln (Central).

Paul D. Shannon

Plate 164 (left): Household coal is unloaded from three HTV wagons at Lincoln East Coal Concentration Depot, as Class 47 No. 47380 passes by with 6E44, the 08.31 Colwick Estate to Lindsey Oil Refinery empty tank train.

Paul D. Shannon

Plate 165 (right): Hardly a taxing load for Class 08 shunter No. 08242, as it propels its single oil tank and brake van into the diesel multiple unit depot sidings at Lincoln on 26th July 1984.

Paul D. Shannon

Plate 166: Lincoln Cathedral sets the scene on a slightly misty morning in April 1983, as Class 47 No. 47365 heads 6D65, the 08.06 Peterborough to West Burton flyash empties along the avoiding line between Greetwell and Boultham junctions. This section of line was closed on 14th November of the same year.

Paul D. Shannon

Plate 167: Class 31 No. 31226 pulls out of Lincoln (Central) Station on 13th April 1983 with a southbound ballast train.

Paul D. Shannon

Plate 168 (above): The 07.54 Sheffield to Lincoln (Central) service pauses for custom at Saxilby on 20th June 1981, and is worked by two Class 114 two car diesel multiple units.

Paul D. Shannon

Plate 169 (below): Class 47 No. 47292 heads 6M57, the 08.30 Humber Oil Refinery to Kingsbury working, past Holton-le-Moor, between Market Rasen and Barnetby, on 12th April 1983.

Paul D. Shannon

Plate 170 (above): Class 47 No. 47029 shunts 100 ton oil tanks at the BP loading terminal at Gainsborough (Lea Road) on 12th April 1984, before departing with 6V69, the 10.20 working to Llandarcy Oil Refinery.
Paul D. Shannon

Plate 171 (below): The 17.55 Skegness to Sheffield holiday train arrives at Gainsborough (Lea Road) on 24th July 1984, headed by Class 31 No. 31297.
Paul D. Shannon

Gainsborough to Barnetby

Plate 172: Class 31 No. 31323 passes through Gainsborough (Central) Station with 8D07, the 06.28 Belmont to Immingham mixed freight, on 12th April 1984.

Paul D. Shannon

Plate 173: Approaching Blyton, between Gainsborough and Kirton Lindsey, Class 47 No. 47379 heads east with a rake of 100 ton oil tanks, on 12th April 1984.

Paul D. Shannon

SHEFFIELD

Plate 175 (above): Class 56 No. 56005 passes Kirton Lime Sidings with 6D69, the 16.26 Doncaster to Immingham merry-go-round train, conveying coal for export. The PCA cement wagons on the adjacent line would have arrived on the 6E94 overnight service from Earle's Sidings.

Paul D. Shannon

Plate 176 (right): A westbound train of empty HAA wagons approaches Brigg Station on the evening of 12th April 1983, headed by Class 56 No. 56106.

Paul D. Shannon

Plate 174 (left): The line through Kirton Lindsey had only recently been singled when a Class 114 unit, comprising cars E54026 and E53004, was photographed forming the 17.35 Cleethorpes to Sheffield service, on 12th April 1983.

Paul D. Shannon

The Scunthorpe Line

Plate 177: A Class 40 locomotive, No. 40086, speeds through Crowle with 6N64, the 15.30 Immingham to Tyne Yard 'Speedlink' service, on 13th April 1983. This train will connect at Tyne Yard with 6S92, the 15.20 Hull to Aberdeen (Craiginches).

Paul D. Shannon

Plate 178: The 15.45 Doncaster to Cleethorpes diesel multiple unit crosses the River Trent at Althorpe on 1st August 1984, and is worked by a Class 114 unit, comprising cars E54041 and E53010.

Paul D. Shannon

Plate 179: A single Class 20 locomotive, No. 20028, stands in the parcels bay at Scunthorpe Station on 30th May 1980.

Michael Rhodes

Plate 180: Class 56 locomotive, No. 56007, Romanian-built, arrives at Scunthorpe Yard, on 13th July 1984, with 6E94, the 01.25 Severn Tunnel Junction to Immingham 'Speedlink' working. The train consists of one high-capacity ferry van and several rebuilt BDA bogie bolster wagons.

Michael Rhodes

Plate 181: To convey imported iron ore from Immingham Docks to Scunthorpe BSC Works, a fleet of 100 ton bogie tippler wagons was constructed in 1970, authorised for running at speeds up to 60m.p.h. Here, Class 37 locomotives Nos. 37252 and 37221 leave the BSC ore terminal with a train of empties returning to Immingham.

Paul D. Shannon

Plate 183 (above): The importance of the Normanby Park branch has declined in recent years, in line with the general recession in the steel industry. On 11th April 1984, Class 20 No. 20052 approaches Crosby Mines with the only train of the day — a rake of 18 KRV coil wagons, bound for Flixborough Wharf.

Paul D. Shannon

Plate 184 (right): Class 20 No. 20093 passes Dawes Lane Crossing, Scunthorpe, with the 9T49 trip working from Normanby Park to Scunthorpe West Yard, on 30th May 1980.

Michael Rhodes

Plate 182 (left): Class 31 locomotives Nos. 31232 and 31205 head 6L33, the 13.27 Lindsey Oil Refinery to Leeds ORT working, past Scunthorpe Foreign Ore Branch Junction on 13th April 1983.

Paul D. Shannon

Plate 185: Passing a typical Great Central Railway signal box at Appleby, east of Scunthorpe, the 12.10 Cleethorpes to Manchester (Piccadilly) service is worked by a Class 123/4 unit, comprising cars E51960, E59833, E59766 and E51961, on 13th April 1983.

Paul D. Shannon

Plate 186: In 1984, a Class 114 unit was repainted in the South Yorkshire PTE livery of brown and cream, to commemorate the first ten years of the Passenger Transport Executive. Here, cars E53045 and E54004 are seen leaving Elsham with the 16.40 Doncaster to Cleethorpes service, on 11th April 1984.

Paul D. Shannon

Plate 187 (above right): The 13.45 Immingham to Wolverhampton Steel Terminal special coil train, (6Z16) draws to a halt alongside a fine array of sempahore signals at Wrawby Junction on 1st August 1984. The locomotive is Class 31 No. 31163.

Paul D. Shannon

Plate 188 (right): Class 37 locomotives Nos. 37161 and 37202 head an eastbound train of empty PTA iron ore tipplers through Barnetby Station on 12th April 1983.

Paul D. Shannon

Plate 189: Class 56 No. 56112 rounds the curve into Barnetby Station, on 12th April 1983, with 6L56, the 12.05 Immingham to Healey Mills merry-go-round empties.

Paul D. Shannon

Plate 190: Class 55 'Deltic' locomotives could occasionally be seen on through workings between London (King's Cross) and Cleethorpes, although the majority of trains were worked by Class 47 locomotives. On 5th June 1980, Class 55 'Deltic' No. 55019 *Royal Highland Fusilier* pauses at Barnetby with the 13.13 departure from Cleethorpes.

Paul D. Shannon

Plate 191: Passing a rare example of a gallows signal at Barnetby East, Class 47 No 47041 heads west with an oil train from Immingham, on 4th September 1979.
Les Nixon

Plate 192: Class 31/4 No. 31434 passes Croxton Lime Works, east of Barnetby, with the 12.43 Cleethorpes to Manchester (Piccadilly) working, on 1st August 1984. Locomotive-hauled formations replaced the Class 123/4 diesel multiple units on this route in May of the same year.
Paul D. Shannon

Plate 193: With colour light signals already in position to replace the existing semaphores, Class 47 No. 47223 enters Brocklesby Station on 12th April 1983, with 6L33, the 13.27 Lindsey Oil Refinery to Leeds ORT working.

Paul D. Shannon

Plate 194: The 07.00 Sheffield to Cleethorpes diesel multiple unit approaches Brocklesby on 1st August 1984, formed of Class 114 cars E53031 and E54034.

Paul D. Shannon

Plate 195: Wooden level crossing gates close behind the 14.43 Cleethorpes to Doncaster diesel multiple unit as it pulls out of Habrough Station on 5th June 1980. Notice the unusual junction layout beyond the station — this has since been replaced by the more standard arrangement of two straight main lines, with single leads for access to the New Holland branch.

Paul D. Shannon

Plate 196: Cravens diesel multiple unit cars, E51284 and E56445, stand at the desolate terminus at Barton-on-Humber, having worked an afternoon service from New Holland Pier.

Paul D. Shannon

To New Holland . . .

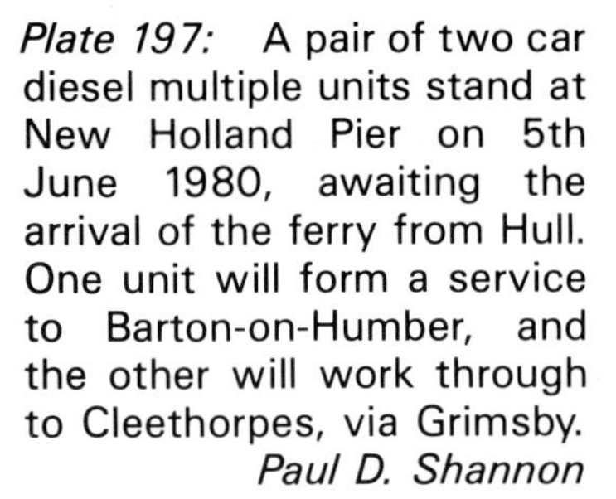

Plate 197: A pair of two car diesel multiple units stand at New Holland Pier on 5th June 1980, awaiting the arrival of the ferry from Hull. One unit will form a service to Barton-on-Humber, and the other will work through to Cleethorpes, via Grimsby.
Paul D. Shannon

Plate 198: Some of the longest surviving Great Central lower quadrant signals were those at New Holland Town, controlling the triangle which closed in 1981 with the opening of the Humber Bridge. Here, a Class 105 unit, comprising cars E51284 and E56445, is seen heading for Barton-on-Humber on an afternoon service from New Holland Pier.
Paul D. Shannon

Plate 199: After the introduction of through trains between Cleethorpes and Barton-on-Humber, a Class 114 unit, comprising cars E53032 and E54016, is seen at Thornton Abbey Halt with the 15.00 departure from Barton-on-Humber, on 12th April 1983.
Paul D. Shannon

Plate 200: Class 47 No. 47142 heads 6D78, the 15.00 Immingham to Belmont 'Speedlink' service, through Ulceby on 12th April 1983.

Paul D. Shannon

Plate 201: With Lindsey Oil Refinery standing on the horizon, and the Humber Oil Refinery branch leading off to the right, Class 56 No. 56106 heads west from Immingham with 6D43, the 15.45 merry-go-round empties to Worksop.

Paul D. Shannon

Plate 202: Class 08 shunters, Nos. 08242 and 08393 are pictured, on 13th September 1979, at Immingham Reception Sidings.

Les Nixon

Plate 203: This line-up at Immingham motive power depot was photographed on 13th July 1984, with locomotives Nos. 56109, 56114, 56026, 37153 and 37252 present.

Michael Rhodes

Grimsby and Cleethorpes

Plate 204: Grimsby West Marsh Yard was virtually empty on 12th April 1983, when Class 31 No. 31195 was photographed trundling up the centre siding on its way to Immingham Depot. There seems little work for Class 08 shunter No. 08743 to do!

Paul D. Shannon

Plate 205: The 11.15 Newark (North Gate) to Cleethorpes diesel multiple unit approaches Grimsby Town on 11th April 1984, worked by a Class 114 unit, comprising cars E53018 and E54033.

Paul D. Shannon

Plate 206: Class 105 cars E51284 and E56446 form the 09.25 Doncaster to Cleethorpes service on 12th April 1983, and are seen passing Wellowgate Crossing at the west end of Grimsby Town Station. This stretch of line is well-known for its profusion of level crossings — there are no less than four of them within half a mile of each other!
Paul D. Shannon

Plate 207: Class 31 locomotives now operate regularly into Cleethorpes from both Manchester and Newark. On 11th April 1984, the 12.07 service from Newark (North Gate) arrives at its destination behind Class 31/4 No. 31436.
Paul D. Shannon